UNITED METHODIST CHURCH
OF UNIONTOWN
13370 Cleveland Ave., N.W.
Uniontown, Ohio 44685

People of the Bible

The Bible through stories and pictures

Jesus Begins
His Work

Copyright © in this format Belitha Press Ltd., 1982

Illustrations copyright © Chris Molan 1982

Art Director: Treld Bicknell

First published in the United States of America 1982
by Raintree Publishers, Inc.
205 West Highland Avenue, Milwaukee, Wisconsin 53203
in association with Belitha Press Ltd, London.

Conceived, designed and produced by Belitha Press Ltd,
40 Belitha Villas, London NI IPD

Moody Press Edition 1983
ISBN: 0-8024-0394-8

First published in Australia in paperback 1982
by Princeton Books Pty Ltd, PO Box 24, Cheltenham, Victoria 3192
in association with Raintree Childrens Books
205 West Highland Avenue, Milwaukee, Wisconsin 53203

ISBN 0 909091 18 8 (Australian)

Jesus Begins His Work

RETOLD BY ELLA K. LINDVALL
PICTURES BY CHRIS MOLAN

MOODY PRESS
CHICAGO

Every year Mary and Joseph used to go to Jerusalem for a time called the feast of the Passover. When Jesus was twelve years old, He went with them.

When the feasting was over, Mary and Joseph started on the long journey back home to Nazareth. Jesus wasn't with them. They thought He was walking with some other relatives and friends.

But He wasn't. Jesus was still in Jerusalem.
And Mary and Joseph walked all day before
they discovered He had been left behind.

There was nothing to do but go back. So
they did.

Where would Jesus be? At the market? No, not there. After looking a long time, Mary and Joseph found Him. He was in the Temple.

He was talking to the wise teachers, who couldn't understand how a boy only twelve years old could know so much. (They didn't know that Jesus was God's Son.)

Mary said to Him, "How could You do this to us? We've been terribly worried about You."

Jesus gently answered, "Didn't you know I had to be in My heavenly Father's house?"

Then He went back to Nazareth with Mary and Joseph and did what they told Him.

Many years later some people thought John the Baptist might be the Special One whom God had promised to send.

John said, "I'm not the one. But He is coming soon. I have seen Him, and I know He is the Son of God."

John the Baptist was talking about Jesus.

One day, John was with two of his followers when he saw Jesus coming. He said, "Look! There is the Lamb of God."

When Andrew heard that, he left John and followed Jesus. Later he said to his brother, Simon Peter, "Come and see. We have found the Christ, God's Special One."

Then Andrew brought Simon Peter to Jesus.

Next Jesus found Philip, who went with Him, too. All these men were called the disciples of Jesus.

Besides Andrew and Simon Peter and Philip, there were James and John, Matthew and Bartholomew, Thomas and Simon, James the son of Alphaeus, Thaddeus, and Judas Iscariot.

They went with Jesus everywhere.

One day there was a wedding party in a little town called Cana. Mary and Jesus and His disciples had been invited.

After the party had gone on for a while, Mary heard some bad news. The wine was all gone. Now there was nothing for people to drink.

Mary said to Jesus, "There's no more wine for the guests to drink." She said to the servants, "Whatever my son tells you, you should do."

Jesus told the servants to fill six big jars with water. Then He said, "Now pour something to drink from one of those jars and take it to the headwaiter."

When the servants did that, they saw that the water had been turned into wine! They gave the headwaiter some first. He said this wine was even better than the wine they had drunk before.

That was the first wonderful thing Jesus did to show He is God's Son.

After that, Jesus did many more miracles.

He was teaching in a house full of people one day, when a man who couldn't walk was lowered through the roof down to where Jesus was.

First, Jesus told him, "Your sins are forgiven." Then He said, "Get up, roll up your blanket, and go home."

At once the man was well and walked out of the house. All the people watched, greatly surprised. They said, "We never saw anything like this before."

Another time, a blind man was brought to Jesus. The man's friends said, "Please touch him so that he can see."

Jesus made his eyes well, and the man who had been blind went happily home.

Then, an important man named Jairus came to see Jesus. "My little daughter is dying," he said. "Please come."

Jesus went to Jairus's house. He found everyone crying, for the little girl had already died. But Jesus went inside and took her by the hand. "Child, get up," He said.

At once the little girl stood up, alive and well.

Jesus and His disciples traveled to many places. Many people listened to Jesus teach about God and how to please Him. They saw the wonderful things that Jesus did. And many said, "Truly, Jesus is the Son of God."

Moody Press, a ministry of the Moody Bible Institute, is designed for education, evangelization, and edification. If we may assist you in knowing more about Christ and the Christian life, please write us without obligation: Moody Press, c/o MLM, Chicago, Illinois 60610.

The Land of the Bible Today

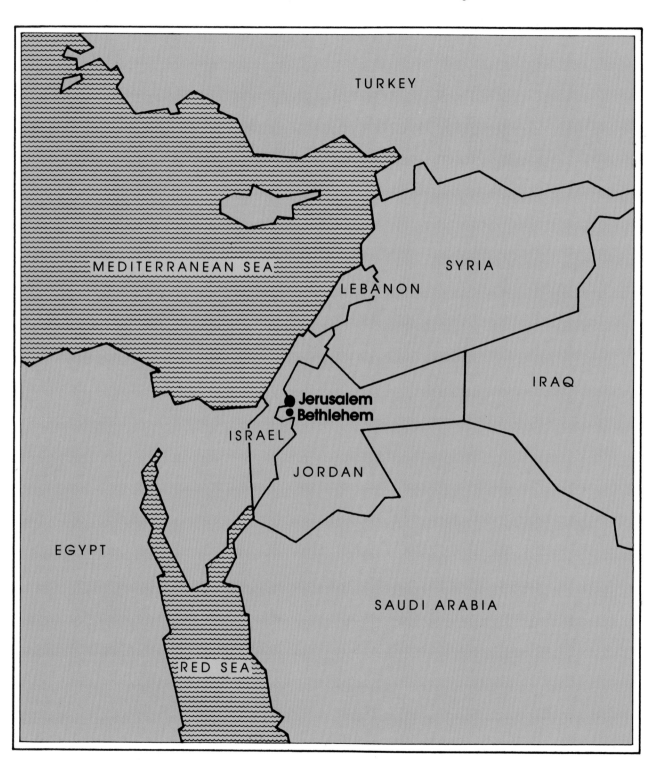

TURKEY

MEDITERRANEAN SEA

SYRIA

LEBANON

IRAQ

● Jerusalem
● Bethlehem

ISRAEL

JORDAN

EGYPT

SAUDI ARABIA

RED SEA